Poetry for Young People

William Wordsworth

Edited by Alan Liu
Illustrated by James Muir

Sterling Publishing Co., Inc.
New York

For my daughter, Lian, age 10
—Alan Liu

For my dad James
—James Muir

Published by Sterling Publishing Co., Inc.
387 Park Avenue South, New York, NY 10016
Text © 2003 by Alan Liu
Illustrations © 2003 by James Muir
Portrait of William Wordsworth by Henry Edridge on page 4
courtesy of Dove Cottage, The Wordsworth Trust
Selections from *The Prelude* 1799, 1805, 1850 in *William Wordsworth:
A Norton Critical Edition,* edited by Jonathan Wordsworth, et al.
Copyright © 1979 by W.W. Norton & Company, Inc.
Used by permission of W.W. Norton & Company, Inc.
Distributed in Canada by Sterling Publishing
℅ Canadian Manda Group, One Atlantic Avenue, Suite 105
Toronto, Ontario, Canada M6K 3E7
Distributed in Great Britain and Europe by Chris Lloyd
at Orca Book Services, Stanley House, Fleets Lane, Poole BH15 3AJ, England
Distributed in Australia by Capricorn Link (Australia) Pty. Ltd.
P.O. Box 704, Windsor, NSW 2756 Australia

Sterling ISBN 0-8069-8277-2

CONTENTS

INTRODUCTION

He loved to walk alone among the mountains, lakes, and wilds of the Lake District in England, his home. Sometimes it was as if there was no one else in the world, and he would look at the way the light fell on a tree or the wind came through the grasses as if they had something secret to tell him. Many times, he would write his poetry outside while walking—write it aloud without pen or paper.

But nature was only complete for him when shared with a few, special people. Once, at a time when he was writing some of his best poetry, he and his friends carved their initials on a large rock. "W.W." it said at the top, and then beneath: "M.H., D.W., S.T.C., J.W., S.H."

His name was William Wordsworth, and the other initials carved on the rock were those of his beloved younger sister Dorothy and younger brother John, his future wife Mary Hutchinson and her sister Sara, and his best friend and fellow poet, Samuel Taylor Coleridge. William, Coleridge, and Dorothy (who described their life in her famous journals) were at the heart of a new movement in poetry called Romanticism—a movement of strong "feeling" and "imagination" inspired by nature, the lives of common people, and often the poets' own lives. Even John, who captained a ship at sea, was what William called a "silent poet" who shared their interests.

William was born on April 7, 1770, in the Lake District, a land in the northwest of England famous for its mountain and lake scenery, its small towns, and its simple way of life. Many people farmed or raised sheep there. William's father was a lawyer who was often away from home on business for the biggest landowner in the area. His mother let William and his brothers (one older, two younger) and his sister play by themselves much of the time among the fields, streams, and hills outside their house in the town of Cockermouth. Those were happy, carefree days when William and Dorothy played at chasing butterflies (see page 12, "To a Butterfly").

But then tragedy came to the family. When William was seven, his mother suddenly became sick with pneumonia and died. Near the end, he walked quietly past the door to her bedroom and saw her sitting still in her easy chair. That was the last time he saw her. Afterwards, his father was very sad and did not know how he could take care of all five of the children by himself.

Dorothy was sent to some relatives in another part of England (it would be many years before William would see her again). The boys went to a boarding school in Hawkshead, a little town in the middle of the Lake District where a kindly woman named Ann Tyson gave them a place to stay and took care of them almost as if they were her own children. They only went home to their father twice a year for holidays.

But death had not yet finished with the family. When William was 13, his father lost his way on one of his business travels and slept outside all night at Christmas time on a cold hillside. He became very sick and soon died, too. Now the children were really alone in the world. Other relatives in the area took care of the boys, but their Uncle Kit was very strict and did not think much of the children's free-spirited ways, especially William's. "Many a time have William, John, Christopher, [another of their brothers] and myself shed tears together, tears of the bitterest sorrow," Dorothy wrote to a friend, "we all of us, each day, feel more sensibly the loss we sustained when we were deprived of our parents…"

It was from this time on, perhaps, that William truly learned about loneliness ("solitude," he called it in his poetry) and how to make something good from it. When he was alone he was free to imagine and feel things that others didn't. And he learned, too, that he was never really alone when he had nature around him. The mountains, lakes, woods, and winds were like a ghost family to him. Sometimes he even felt they had a hidden "spirit" that guided him like a mother or father. In the poem he later wrote about his life called *The Prelude*, he remembered that it was these childhood years—in both their joy and sorrow—that made him a poet. He remembered the times he ran out like "a naked savage" into thundershowers, bathed in streams, climbed cliffs to steal birds' eggs, skated under the stars at night, and even once stole a rowboat for a ride on a lake (see pages 36–38, "The Stolen Boat"). "Fair seed-time had my soul," he said. And he remembered, too, all the sad and scary times in those years—like the time just after stealing the boat when a giant, dark mountain seemed to chase after him, or the "stormy, and rough, and wild" day when he waited on a hilltop to go home to his father from school just before his father died.

William wrote his first poems while at school in Hawkshead. He had a talent for it. But when he went away to college at Cambridge University, his guardian uncles thought he should study hard and take a position (become a "fellow") at the university or perhaps become a lawyer. But William did not do especially well in college. Instead, he read freely in many subjects (he was especially fascinated by geometry), and continued writing poetry. Coming home to the Lake District during the summers, he would walk alone in the hills with his dog, a terrier, and compose poems aloud. The dog barked if anyone was coming, and he would stop so as not to seem crazy.

Then, in the summer before he graduated from college, William went to Europe with a friend and walked through France, Switzerland, and northern Italy with just the clothes on his back and a knapsack. It was an exciting time. The French Revolution had just begun a year before in 1789. Many poor and middle-class French people joined with writers, philosophers, lawyers, and politicians to rebel against the old France of aristocrats ruled by King Louis XVI. They wanted to start a democracy like that in America (the American Revolution had taken place just about a dozen years earlier).

At this time, though, William was mainly a tourist: he was impressed by the scenery of the Swiss mountains. But his feelings about the French Revolution soon deepened. After graduating from college—and while still very unsure about what to do with his life—he returned by himself to France. Here he met a young, well-educated revolutionary named Michel Beaupuy who helped him learn what the Revolution was about. Before long, he found himself siding strongly with the revolutionaries, becoming a "patriot of the people." And something else important happened, too. For the first time, he fell in love. She was a young French woman named Annette Vallon, and soon the two would have a baby.

But then things went badly wrong. The French Revolution changed into something William had nightmares about. The "Terror" started. This was the time when the revolutionaries used the guillotine to cut off the heads of many French people and finally the French king and queen. Many thousands of people lost their lives, and France went to war with the rest of Europe and England.

Meanwhile, William and Annette's love seemed doomed. Though they very much wanted to marry, they were not able to. After all, he was a penniless young man from another country. At last, William returned to England without Annette. She gave birth to their child without him, and it would be ten years before he saw their daughter for the first time (see page 31, "It is a Beauteous Evening, Calm and Free").

Back in England, William was very unhappy. It seemed like the end of the world. All his hopes for the French Revolution were at an end. (Sometimes he woke up with nightmares about France.) He couldn't even write a letter to Annette because the war between England and France had cut off the mail between the two countries. And meanwhile, he still didn't know what to do with his life.

In the next few years while he lived here and there in London and other places in England, William wrote poems and even a play (a tragedy) about all the pain and suffering in the world. But these poems borrowed from the way other poets wrote. He had not yet found his own voice as a poet.

Finally, life became better. William came to accept the fact that the French Revolution had not turned out the way he wanted. And, though he would not see Annette again except for once or twice many years later, his personal life became happier. His sister Dorothy, who was separated from him when their mother died, came to live with him again. They were inseparable from this time on—walking together, reading books together, and working on his poems together (often she would write down his verses).

In 1799, the two moved into a small house in Grasmere—a little town in the Lake District on the shores of a beautiful lake with a perfect little island in the middle. The house was called Dove Cottage (it still exists today, with the Wordsworth Museum near it). They would live at Dove Cottage for many years. When William later married Mary Hutchinson—a friend both he and Dorothy had known since their youth—she came to live with them in Dove Cottage, too. Meeting Coleridge was another very important event in his life at this time. The two poets discovered how close they were in their beliefs and feelings. They became each other's teachers of poetry.

Finally, another event improved William's life in a practical way. A well-to-do friend, who believed in William's talents as a poet, died and left in his will a small sum of money for him—enough to free him to write poetry without worrying about making a living doing something else.

The conditions were now right. With the help of Coleridge and Dorothy, William found a way to make a new kind of poetry that was truly his own—that came out of who he was and what he had lived through. His poetry, he discovered, would be about ordinary people. The French Revolution had promised power to "the People," but William now felt that the ordinary farmers and shepherds he lived among in the Lake District were the true "people."

He would write about them—about what they thought and felt during the great events of their life: childhood, friendship, work, and death. So, too, his poetry would be about his own everyday self—about his thoughts and feelings as he grew up to be a poet. And above all, he would write about nature—about the mountains, lakes, and wilds that brought out the best in people.

William became the first poet of the "ordinary." He believed that country folk, his own life, and nature were every bit as magical as all the gods and devils, kings and queens, and elegant city people that earlier poets wrote about. Even little children, the subject of many of his best poems, were in their way greater than any king or queen.

In 1798, when he was 28, William published his famous *Lyrical Ballads,* a book of poems that included a few by Coleridge as well. Two years later, he published the book again with additional poems. The "Preface" to *Lyrical Ballads* explained what his poetry was about. He wanted, he said, "to choose incidents and situations from common life" and to describe them in a way that gave them "a certain colouring of imagination, whereby ordinary things should be presented to the mind in an unusual way…"

William continued writing and publishing poetry. At first, some people did not understand his work or thought it was about things that were too ordinary or common. But as the years passed, his poetry was read by more and more people who felt deeply what he was trying to say. By 1815, he was able to publish his first collected edition (a book that "collected" or gathered together the poems he had written up to that time).

Sad things happened to him, too. His brother John died at sea when his ship sank in a storm. William's grief was sharp and deep. "The set is now broken," he said, meaning that the set of his brothers and sisters was now incomplete. Later, two of the five children William had with Mary died when they were very young (see p. 34, "Surprised By Joy").

When William himself died in 1850 at the old age of 80, he had become one of the most important poets of his time and the poet laureate of England (the writer named by the British monarch as England's national poet). And people did not even know until he died that he had been saving up his greatest poem. It was called *The Prelude*, and it was about his childhood and the way he grew up to be a poet (see pages 35–42).

However famous William became, though, there was still something lonely about him. He and his friends had a habit of naming places in nature for each other—special rocks, woods, and so on. There was one mountain in the Lake District that seemed the "loneliest place we have among the clouds." Dorothy named the mountain after him.

I.
NATURE

Then, dearest Maiden, move along these shades
In gentleness of heart; with gentle hand
Touch—for there is a spirit in the woods.
—from "Nutting"

I WANDERED LONELY AS A CLOUD

The poet's sister, Dorothy, wrote in her journal one day after the two of them took a walk by Ullswater Lake: "I never saw daffodils so beautiful, they grew among the mossy stones about and about them, some rested their heads upon these stones, as on a pillow, for weariness and the rest tossed and reeled and danced and seemed as if they verily laughed with the wind…" This is the poem that William made of the daffodils. The poet imagines that he is "lonely." But the "crowd" and "company" of the daffodils make for a busy, social vision of nature's beauty—almost as if the poet really were at a "dance."

I wandered lonely as a cloud
That floats on high o'er vales and hills,
When all at once I saw a crowd,
A host, of golden daffodils;
Beside the lake, beneath the trees,
Fluttering and dancing in the breeze.

Continuous as the stars that shine
And twinkle on the milky way,
They stretched in never-ending line
Along the margin of a bay:
Ten thousand saw I at a glance,
Tossing their heads in sprightly dance.

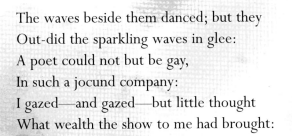

The waves beside them danced; but they
Out-did the sparkling waves in glee:
A poet could not but be gay,
In such a jocund company:
I gazed—and gazed—but little thought
What wealth the show to me had brought:

For oft, when on my couch I lie
In vacant or in pensive mood,
They flash upon that inward eye
Which is the bliss of solitude;
And then my heart with pleasure fills,
And dances with the daffodils.

vale—*valley*
host—*large group, crowd*
jocund—*merry, joyful*
pensive—*thoughtful*

TO A BUTTERFLY

Dorothy notes in her journal:"William…wrote the Poem to a Butterfly! He ate not a morsel, nor put on his stockings but sate with his shirt neck unbuttoned, and his waistcoat open while he did it. The thought first came upon him as we were talking about the pleasure we both always feel at the sight of a Butterfly." In his poetry, William sometimes used the name "Emmeline" for his sister, Dorothy.

Stay near me—do not take thy flight!
A little longer stay in sight!
Much converse do I find in thee,
Historian of my infancy!
Float near me; do not yet depart!
Dead times revive in thee:
Thou bring'st, gay creature as thou art!
A solemn image to my heart,
My father's family!

Oh! pleasant, pleasant were the days,
The time, when in our childish plays,
My sister Emmeline and I
Together chased the butterfly!
A very hunter did I rush
Upon the prey;—with leaps and springs
I followed on from brake to bush;
But she, God loves her! feared to brush
The dust from off its wings.

converse—*familiarity, shared feelings, talk*
brake—*thicket, underbrush*

INSCRIPTIONS SUPPOSED TO BE FOUND
IN AND NEAR A HERMIT'S CELL, 1818
III

This poem was the third of five that Wordsworth published as a group titled "Inscriptions Supposed to be Found in and near a Hermit's Cell, 1818." An inscription is a poem carved or written on a tree, bench, stone, or other object, often in a natural setting. Here, the poet contrasts the way the bubbles under the ice disappear so quickly with the thoughts that an inscription tries to carve permanently onto the scene.

Hast thou seen, with flash incessant,
Bubbles gliding under ice,
Bodied forth and evanescent,
No one knows by what device?

Such are thoughts!—A wind-swept meadow
Mimicking a troubled sea,
Such is life; and death a shadow
From the rock eternity!

incessant—*unceasing, without stop*
evanescent—*quickly vanishing*

13

LINES WRITTEN IN EARLY SPRING

Wordsworth's nature poems are often about the difficult to understand relation between people and nature. Sometimes, as when the poet feels the thrilling pleasure of the birds here, he thinks nature is linked to the human soul. But at other times, when he thinks about the suffering and unfairness humanity has brought on itself, he feels there is a great distance between the simple things of nature and people.

I heard a thousand blended notes,
While in a grove I sate reclined,
In that sweet mood when pleasant thoughts
Bring sad thoughts to the mind.

To her fair works did Nature link
The human soul that through me ran;
And much it grieved my heart to think
What man has made of man.

Through primrose tufts, in that green bower,
The periwinkle trailed its wreaths;
And 'tis my faith that every flower
Enjoys the air it breathes.

The birds around me hopped and played,
Their thoughts I cannot measure:—
But the least motion which they made
It seemed a thrill of pleasure.

The budding twigs spread out their fan,
To catch the breezy air;
And I must think, do all I can,
That there was pleasure there.

If this belief from heaven be sent,
If such be Nature's holy plan,
Have I not reason to lament
What man has made of man?

sate—*sat*

MY HEART LEAPS UP WHEN I BEHOLD

Do you remember the first time you saw the arc of a rainbow and wondered where it touched the ground, or how its colors could blur so smoothly into each other? Whether he is young or old, Wordsworth says, he will remember.

My heart leaps up when I behold
    A rainbow in the sky:
So was it when my life began;
So is it now I am a man;
So be it when I shall grow old,
    Or let me die!
The Child is father of the Man;
I could wish my days to be
Bound each to each by natural piety.

piety—*devotion, faithfulness*

II.
CHILDREN & YOUNG PEOPLE

O blessed vision! happy child!
Thou art so exquisitely wild,
I think of thee with many fears
For what may be thy lot in future years.
—from "To H. C., Six Years Old"

THE REVERIE OF POOR SUSAN

Susan lives in London now and is homesick for the countryside. For just a moment in the still morning, when she hears a bird singing in its cage, she thinks of the place where she grew up. For just that moment, it is almost as if the mountains, trees, and mists of the Lake District were there with her in the city.

At the corner of Wood Street, when daylight appears,
Hangs a Thrush that sings loud, it has sung for three
        years:
Poor Susan has passed by the spot, and has heard
In the silence of morning the song of the Bird.

'Tis a note of enchantment; what ails her? She sees
A mountain ascending, a vision of trees;
Bright volumes of vapour through Lothbury glide,
And a river flows on through the vale of Cheapside.

Green pastures she views in the midst of the dale,
Down which she so often has tripped with her pail;
And a single small cottage, a nest like a dove's,
The one only dwelling on earth that she loves.

She looks, and her heart is in heaven: but they fade,
The mist and the river, the hill and the shade:
The stream will not flow, and the hill will not rise,
And the colours have all passed away from her eyes!

Wood Street, Lothbury, Cheapside—*streets in a trade
    district of London*
tripped—*walked or skipped with light, quick steps*

18

A SLUMBER DID MY SPIRIT SEAL

Wordsworth wrote several poems about a young girl who died named Lucy ("No motion has she now, no force"). He made her up. There was no particular child named Lucy, yet in another sense she is more real than anything for the poet. Wordsworth grew up at a time when between one-fourth and one-third of English children died before they were fifteen. The quickness and brightness of life that the poet celebrates is often balanced against a sense of just how precious and fragile life is.

A slumber did my spirit seal;
   I had no human fears:
She seemed a thing that could not feel
   The touch of earthly years.

No motion has she now, no force;
   She neither hears nor sees;
Rolled round in earth's diurnal course,
   With rocks, and stones, and trees.

diurnal course—*daily rotation*

LUCY GRAY: OR, SOLITUDE

Have you ever looked over your shoulder to answer a friend you thought had called you, only to find that no one was there? It was only the wind or something else? That is the feeling the poet is trying to capture in this poem, but in a more haunting way. Lucy Gray fell off a bridge and died in the cold stream. But sometimes it seems as if she were still here, singing, just outside of sight.

Oft I had heard of Lucy Gray:
And, when I crossed the wild,
I chanced to see at break of day
   The solitary child.

No mate, no comrade Lucy knew;
She dwelt on a wide moor,
  —The sweetest thing that ever grew
Beside a human door!

You yet may spy the fawn at play,
The hare upon the green;
But the sweet face of Lucy Gray
Will never more be seen.

"To-night will be a stormy night—
You to the town must go;
And take a lantern, Child, to light
Your mother through the snow."

"That, Father! will I gladly do:
'Tis scarcely afternoon—
The minster-clock has just struck two,
And yonder is the moon!"

At this the Father raised his hook,
And snapped a faggot-band;
He plied his work;—and Lucy took
The lantern in her hand.

wild—*open uncultivated area,*
   wilderness
minster-clock—*church clock*
faggot-band—*bundle of twigs or*
   sticks, which can be lit as a
   lantern
plied his work—*applied himself*
   to his work, worked hard

Not blither is the mountain roe:
With many a wanton stroke
Her feet disperse the powdery snow,
That rises up like smoke.

The storm came on before its time:
She wandered up and down;
And many a hill did Lucy climb:
But never reached the town.

The wretched parents all that night
Went shouting far and wide;
But there was neither sound nor sight
To serve them for a guide.

At day-break on a hill they stood
That overlooked the moor;
And thence they saw the bridge of wood,
A furlong from their door.

They wept— and, turning homeward, cried,
"In heaven we all shall meet;"
—When in the snow the mother spied
The print of Lucy's feet.

Then downwards from the steep hill's edge
They tracked the footmarks small;
And through the broken hawthorn hedge,
And by the long stone-wall;

And then an open field they crossed:
The marks were still the same;
They tracked them on, nor ever lost;
And to the bridge they came.

They followed from the snowy bank
Those footmarks, one by one,
Into the middle of the plank;
And further there were none!

—Yet some maintain that to this day
She is a living child;
That you may see sweet Lucy Gray
Upon the lonesome wild.

O'er rough and smooth she trips along,
And never looks behind;
And sings a solitary song
That whistles in the wind.

blither—*happier, more free of cares*
wanton—*unrestrained, high-spirited*
disperse—*scatter*
roe—*the roe deer, a small European deer*
furlong—*a measure of distance, about*
    an eighth of a mile

THE SOLITARY REAPER

Wordsworth felt that the simple people living closest to nature—the people who work the fields or tend the sheep—are like natural poets. They feel strongly and speak plainly. He thought of the nightingale, too, as a kind of natural poet. Here, he combines these ideas in the solitary reaper whom he likens to a nightingale. He doesn't understand what the girl is singing because her language is Erse, the old language of Scotland. But perhaps for that very reason her song, like the best poetry, haunts him with imaginative possibilities.

Behold her, single in the field,
Yon solitary Highland Lass!
Reaping and singing by herself;
Stop here, or gently pass!
Alone she cuts and binds the grain,
And sings a melancholy strain;
O listen! for the Vale profound
Is overflowing with the sound.

No Nightingale did ever chaunt
More welcome notes to weary bands
Of travellers in some shady haunt,
Among Arabian sands:
A voice so thrilling ne'er was heard
In spring-time from the Cuckoo-bird,
Breaking the silence of the seas
Among the farthest Hebrides.

Will no one tell me what she sings?—
Perhaps the plaintive numbers flow
For old, unhappy, far-off things,
And battles long ago:
Or is it some more humble lay,
Familiar matter of to-day?
Some natural sorrow, loss, or pain,
That has been, and may be again?

Whate'er the theme, the Maiden sang
As if her song could have no ending;
I saw her singing at her work,
And o'er the sickle bending;—
I listened, motionless and still;
And, as I mounted up the hill,
The music in my heart I bore,
Long after it was heard no more.

Reaper—*one who reaps or cuts grain for harvest with a scythe or sickle*
Highland Lass—*girl from the highlands or mountains of Scotland*
Vale—*valley*
chaunt—*old form of the word "chant"*
Hebrides—*islands off the coast of Scotland*
plaintive—*sorrowful, mournful*
lay—*song*

ALICE FELL: OR, POVERTY

Sometimes children cry hard and long because of something that has happened and there is no way their parents can make the hurt go away except just by holding them and waiting. But Alice Fell has no parents. How much worse must it hurt when something happens to her!

The post-boy drove with fierce career,
For threatening clouds the moon had drowned;
When, as we hurried on, my ear
Was smitten with a startling sound.

As if the wind blew many ways,
I heard the sound,—and more and more;
It seemed to follow with the chaise,
And still I heard it as before.

At length I to the boy called out;
He stopped his horses at the word,
But neither cry, nor voice, nor shout,
Nor aught else like it, could be heard.

The boy then smacked his whip, and fast
The horses scampered through the rain;
But, hearing soon upon the blast
The cry, I bade him halt again.

Forthwith alighting on the ground,
"Whence comes," said I, "this piteous moan?"
And there a little Girl I found,
Sitting behind the chaise, alone.

"My cloak!" no other word she spake,
But loud and bitterly she wept,
As if her innocent heart would break;
And down from off her seat she leapt.

post-boy—*driver of the horse carriage or "chaise"*
with fierce career—*fast, recklessly*
smitten—*struck*

24

"What ails you, child?"—she sobbed "Look here!"
I saw it in the wheel entangled,
A weather-beaten rag as e'er
From any garden scare-crow dangled.

There, twisted between nave and spoke,
It hung, nor could at once be freed;
But our joint pains unloosed the cloak,
A miserable rag indeed!

"And whither are you going, child,
To-night along these lonesome ways?"
"To Durham," answered she, half wild—
"Then come with me into the chaise."

Insensible to all relief
Sat the poor girl, and forth did send
Sob after sob, as if her grief
Could never, never have an end.

"My child, in Durham do you dwell?"
She checked herself in her distress,
And said, "My name is Alice Fell;
I'm fatherless and motherless.

"And I to Durham, Sir, belong."
Again, as if the thought would choke
Her very heart, her grief grew strong;
And all was for her tattered cloak!

The chaise drove on; our journey's end
Was nigh; and, sitting by my side,
As if she had lost her only friend
She wept, nor would be pacified.

nave and spoke—*parts of a carriage wheel (the
    nave is the hub, the spokes go out from the hub
    to the wheel rim)*
our joint pains—*our efforts together*
Durham—*a city in England*

Up to the tavern-door we post;
Of Alice and her grief I told;
And I gave money to the host,
To buy a new cloak for the old.

"And let it be of duffil grey,
As warm a cloak as man can sell!"
Proud creature was she the next day,
The little orphan, Alice Fell!

duffil—*a kind of woolen cloth*

III.
THE PRESENT & THE PAST

How shall I trace the history, where seek
The origin of what I then have felt?
Oft in those moments such a holy calm
Did overspread my soul that I forgot
That I had bodily eyes, and what I saw
Appeared like something in myself, a dream,
A prospect in my mind.
      —from *The Prelude*, Book 2

THE TWO APRIL MORNINGS

When we really think hard about the past, sometimes it almost seems to come alive again in our mind. We cry or we laugh as if the people and things we miss were with us again. Many of Wordsworth's poems are about remembering the past. Memory, he once said, is "emotion recollected in tranquillity."

We walked along, while bright and red
Uprose the morning sun;
And Matthew stopped, he looked, and said,
"The will of God be done!"

A village schoolmaster was he,
With hair of glittering grey;
As blithe a man as you could see
On a spring holiday.

And on that morning, through the grass,
And by the steaming rills,
We travelled merrily, to pass
A day among the hills.

"Our work," said I, "was well begun,
Then, from thy breast what thought,
Beneath so beautiful a sun,
So sad a sigh has brought?"

A second time did Matthew stop;
And fixing still his eye
Upon the eastern mountain-top,
To me he made reply:

"Yon cloud with that long purple cleft
Brings fresh into my mind
A day like this which I have left
Full thirty years behind.

blithe—*happy and carefree*
rills—*small brooks*

"And just above yon slope of corn
Such colours, and no other,
Were in the sky, that April morn,
Of this the very brother.

"With rod and line I sued the sport
Which that sweet season gave,
And, to the churchyard come, stopped short
Beside my daughter's grave.

"Nine summers had she scarcely seen,
The pride of all the vale;
And then she sang;—she would have been
A very nightingale.

"Six feet in earth my Emma lay;
And yet I loved her more,
For so it seemed, than till that day
I e'er had loved before.

"And, turning from her grave, I met,
Beside the churchyard yew,
A blooming Girl, whose hair was wet
With points of morning dew.

"A basket on her head she bare;
Her brow was smooth and white:
To see a child so very fair,
It was a pure delight!

"No fountain from its rocky cave
E'er tripped with foot so free;
She seemed as happy as a wave
That dances on the sea.

"There came from me a sigh of pain
Which I could ill confine;
I looked at her, and looked again:
And did not wish her mine!"

Matthew is in his grave, yet now,
Methinks, I see him stand,
As at that moment, with a bough
Of wilding in his hand.

yew—*an evergreen shrub*
wilding—*a plant like a crab-apple tree that
grows wild but is related to cultivated plants*

COMPOSED UPON WESTMINSTER BRIDGE, SEPTEMBER 3, 1802

On the trip during which he wrote this poem, William rode with his sister in a coach over London's Westminster Bridge toward the coast of England and then to France. He was on his way to visit Annette Vallon, a woman he once loved but had not seen for ten years. It was like a trip to his past. Here he takes a moment to look out the window of his coach and—almost as if he were taking a snapshot—enjoys the powerful beauty of the here and now. (Like "It is a Beauteous Evening, Calm and Fair" and "Surprised By Joy," this poem is a sonnet—a poem with fourteen lines and carefully arranged rhymes.)

Earth has not anything to show more fair:
Dull would he be of soul who could pass by
A sight so touching in its majesty:
This City now doth, like a garment, wear
The beauty of the morning; silent, bare,
Ships, towers, domes, theatres, and temples lie
Open unto the fields, and to the sky;
All bright and glittering in the smokeless air.
Never did sun more beautifully steep
In his first splendour, valley, rock, or hill;
Ne'er saw I, never felt, a calm so deep!
The river glideth at his own sweet will:
Dear God! the very houses seem asleep;
And all that mighty heart is lying still!

The river—the Thames River that runs through London

It Is a Beauteous Evening, Calm and Free

The young girl Wordsworth talks to here is his daughter Caroline. He hardly knows her because he was separated from her and her French mother during the French Revolution (they lived in France, which was at war with England). Here, on a short visit to France during a break in the war, he shares a quiet moment with Caroline at sunset.

It is a beauteous evening, calm and free,
The holy time is quiet as a Nun
Breathless with adoration; the broad sun
Is sinking down in its tranquillity;
The gentleness of heaven broods o'er the Sea:
Listen! the mighty Being is awake,
And doth with his eternal motion make
A sound like thunder—everlastingly.
Dear Child! dear Girl! that walkest with me here,
If thou appear untouched by solemn thought,
Thy nature is not therefore less divine:
Thou liest in Abraham's bosom all the year;
And worshipp'st at the Temple's inner shrine,
God being with thee when we know it not.

Abraham's bosom—*where the innocent and poor find eternal
    comfort (from the Bible, Luke 16:22)*

THE WHITE DOE OF RYLSTONE (EXCERPT)

Wordsworth wrote a long poem called "The White Doe of Rylstone" about a family who fought on the losing side in the Rising of the North in 1569. It was then that the earls of the Northern part of England rebelled against Elizabeth I in an attempt to free Mary Queen of Scots and bring the Catholic religion back to England. This selection is from the beginning of the poem, when the only thing we see of the sad past is an almost magical white deer.

Fast the churchyard fills;—anon
Look again, and they all are gone;
The cluster round the porch, and the folk
Who sate in the shade of the Prior's Oak!
And scarcely have they disappeared
Ere the prelusive hymn is heard:—
With one consent the people rejoice,
Filling the church with a lofty voice!
They sing a service which they feel:
For 'tis the sunrise now of zeal;
Of a pure faith the vernal prime—
In great Eliza's golden time.

A moment ends the fervent din,
And all is hushed, without and within;
For though the priest, more tranquilly,
Recites the holy liturgy,
The only voice which you can hear
Is the river murmuring near.
—When soft!—the dusky trees between,
And down the path through the open green,
Where is no living thing to be seen;
And through yon gateway, where is found,
Beneath the arch with ivy bound,
Free entrance to the churchyard ground—
Comes gliding in with lovely gleam,
Comes gliding in serene and slow,
Soft and silent as a dream,
A solitary Doe!
White she is as lily of June,
And beauteous as the silver moon
When out of sight the clouds are driven

32

And she is left alone in heaven;
Or like a ship some gentle day
In sunshine sailing far away,
A glittering ship, that hath the plain
Of ocean for her own domain.

anon—*now*
Prior—*a church officer*
prelusive—*introductory*
vernal prime—*springtime*
great Eliza—*Elizabeth I, Queen of England*
liturgy—*the rituals of Christian religious ceremonies*

SURPRISED BY JOY

Wordsworth married an English woman named Mary Hutchinson, and they had five children. One of their daughters, Catherine, died from an illness when she was very young. This was a poem for her.

Surprised by joy—impatient as the Wind
I turned to share the transport—Oh! with whom
But Thee, deep buried in the silent tomb,
That spot which no vicissitude can find?
Love, faithful love, recalled thee to my mind—
But how could I forget thee? Through what power,
Even for the least division of an hour,
Have I been so beguiled as to be blind
To my most grievous loss?—That thought's return
Was the worst pang that sorrow ever bore,
Save one, one only, when I stood forlorn,
Knowing my heart's best treasure was no more;
That neither present time, nor years unborn
Could to my sight that heavenly face restore.

transport—*wild emotion*
vicissitude—*change*
beguiled—*fooled*

IV.
Scenes from *The Prelude*

When he was 28 years old, Wordsworth began writing a book-length poem about his own life called The Prelude. *"Prelude" means a beginning or introduction, such as a piece of music that introduces the main music to come. This was Wordsworth's poem about his own beginnings as a poet.*

The following are a few selections from The Prelude *as it existed in its first complete version in 1805 (titles of the selections supplied by the editor). Wordsworth wrote the poem in a form called "blank verse," where the lines are unrhymed "iambic pentameter" (each with ten syllables in a regular meter or rhythm called "iambic").*

> ...The days gone by
> Come back upon me from the dawn almost
> Of life; the hiding-places of my power
> Seem open, I approach, and then they close...
> —from *The Prelude*, Book 11

THE STOLEN BOAT, FROM BOOK 1

When he was a child, it seemed to Wordsworth that Nature guided him directly, like the "muse" that poets long ago believed spoke to them when they were writing poetry. Sometimes Nature spoke gently to him, for example, in the sound of breezes or rivers. But sometimes she spoke hard and gave almost frightening lessons. Here, the young poet takes a boat that doesn't belong to him and rows out on the lake. Suddenly the huge cliff seems to be chasing him but never quite catches him. Such "huge and mighty forms" of Nature haunted his dreams and, later, his poetry.

One evening—surely I was led by her—
I went alone into a shepherd's boat,
A skiff that to a willow-tree was tied
Within a rocky cave, its usual home.
'Twas by the shores of Patterdale, a vale
Wherein I was a stranger, thither come
A schoolboy traveller at the holidays.
Forth rambled from the village inn alone,
No sooner had I sight of this small skiff,
Discovered thus by unexpected chance,
Than I unloosed her tether and embarked.
The moon was up, the lake was shining clear
Among the hoary mountains; from the shore
I pushed, and struck the oars, and struck again
In cadence, and my little boat moved on
Even like a man who moves with stately step
Though bent on speed. It was an act of stealth
And troubled pleasure. Nor without the voice
Of mountain-echoes did my boat move on,
Leaving behind her still on either side
Small circles glittering idly in the moon,
Until they melted all into one track
Of sparkling light. A rocky steep uprose
Above the cavern of the willow-tree,
And now, as suited one who proudly rowed
With his best skill, I fixed a steady view
Upon the top of that same craggy ridge,
The bound of the horizon—for behind
Was nothing but the stars and the grey sky.

skiff—*a small boat*
Patterdale—*a lake in the Lake District of England*
tether—*rope holding the boat to the shore*
hoary—*white with age*
struck the oars—*sank the oars into the water*
cadence—*rhythm, in a timed beat*
act of stealth—*secretive, sneaky act*

She was an elfin pinnace; lustily
I dipped my oars into the silent lake,
And as I rose upon the stroke my boat
Went heaving through the water like a swan—
When from behind that craggy steep, till then
The bound of the horizon, a huge cliff,
As if with voluntary power instinct,
Upreared its head. I struck and struck again,
And, growing still in stature, the huge cliff
Rose up between me and the stars, and still
With measured motion, like a living thing
Strode after me. With trembling hands I turned
And through the silent water stole my way
Back to the cavern of the willow-tree.
There, in her mooring-place I left my bark
And through the meadows homeward went with grave
And serious thoughts; and after I had seen
That spectacle, for many days my brain
Worked with a dim and undetermined sense
Of unknown modes of being. In my thoughts
There was a darkness—call it solitude
Or blank desertion—no familiar shapes
Of hourly objects, images of trees,
Of sea or sky, no colours of green fields,
But huge and mighty forms that do not live
Like living men moved slowly through the mind
By day, and were the trouble of my dreams.

elfin pinnace—*like a fairy boat*
lustily—*eagerly, vigorously*
as if with voluntary power instinct—
    as if under its own power
upreared—*raised up*
measured motion—*timed motion, like*
    the "cadence" of the poet's rowing (see above)

THE BOY OF WINANDER, FROM BOOK 5

Can you whistle through your hands like this? Do you think the owls would answer if you could? In this poem Wordsworth imagines a boy who is the simplest—yet in some ways most powerful—kind of poet: someone who can talk (and listen) to Nature directly.

There was a boy—ye knew him well, ye cliffs
And islands of Winander—many a time
At evening, when the stars had just begun
To move along the edges of the hills,
Rising or setting, would he stand alone
Beneath the trees or by the glimmering lake,
And there, with fingers interwoven, both hands
Pressed closely palm to palm, and to his mouth
Uplifted, he as through an instrument
Blew mimic hootings to the silent owls
That they might answer him. And they would shout
Across the wat'ry vale, and shout again,
Responsive to his call, with quivering peals
And long halloos, and screams, and echoes loud,
Redoubled and redoubled—concourse wild
Of mirth and jocund din. And when it chanced
That pauses of deep silence mocked his skill,
Then sometimes in that silence, while he hung
Listening, a gentle shock of mild surprize
Has carried far into his heart the voice
Of mountain torrents; or the visible scene
Would enter unawares into his mind
With all its solemn imagery, its rocks,
Its woods, and that uncertain heaven, received
Into the bosom of the steady lake.

Winander—*Lake Windermere in the Lake District of England*
concourse—*crowd, gathering*
jocund—*jolly*

Climbing Mt. Snowdon, from Book 13

On a foggy, cloudy night, Wordsworth climbed Mount Snowdon in Wales. When he reached the peak of the mountain, he saw the tops of the clouds spread out below him like a make-believe land hiding the "real sea" beneath. Later, he placed this cloud vision at the end of The Prelude *to stand for what he thought his life as a poet was really about—learning from nature to be imaginative.*

In one of those excursions, travelling then
Through Wales on foot and with a youthful friend,
I left Bethkelet's huts at couching-time,
And westward took my way to see the sun
Rise from the top of Snowdon. Having reached
The cottage at the mountain's foot, we there
Rouzed up the shepherd who by ancient right
Of office is the stranger's usual guide,
And after short refreshment sallied forth.

   It was a summer's night, a close warm night,
Wan, dull, and glaring, with a dripping mist
Low-hung and thick that covered all the sky,
Half threatening storm and rain; but on we went
Unchecked, being full of heart and having faith
In our tried pilot. Little could we see,
Hemmed round on every side with fog and damp,
And, after ordinary travellers' chat
With our conductor, silently we sunk
Each into commerce with his private thoughts.
Thus did we breast the ascent, and by myself
Was nothing either seen or heard the while
Which took me from my musings, save that once
The shepherd's cur did to his own great joy
Unearth a hedgehog in the mountain-crags,
Round which he made a barking turbulent.
This small adventure—for even such it seemed
In that wild place and at the dead of night—
Being over and forgotten, on we wound
In silence as before. With forehead bent

Bethkelet—*town of Beddgelert in Wales*
couching-time—*bed-time*
sallied forth—*ventured out, set out on a journey*
tried pilot—*trusty pilot (that is, the shepherd who guides visitors up the mountain)*
conductor—*guide*
commerce—*exchange, conversation*
cur—*mongrel or mixed-breed dog*
barking turbulent—*rough, noisy barking*

headlands, tongues, and promontory
   shapes—*ridges of land jutting out into the*
   water (here referring to the shapes of the
   clouds)
Usurped upon—*taken over by*
shew—*show*
breach—*gap, chasm, or fracture*

Earthward, as if in opposition set
Against an enemy, I panted up
With eager pace, and no less eager thoughts,
Thus might we wear perhaps an hour away,
Ascending at loose distance each from each,
And I, as chanced, the foremost of the band—
When at my feet the ground appeared to brighten,
And with a step or two seemed brighter still;
Nor had I time to ask the cause of this,
For instantly a light upon the turf
Fell like a flash. I looked about, and lo,
The moon stood naked in the heavens at height
Immense above my head, and on the shore
I found myself of a huge sea of mist,
Which meek and silent rested at my feet.
A hundred hills their dusky backs upheaved
All over this still ocean, and beyond,
Far, far beyond, the vapours shot themselves
In headlands, tongues, and promontory shapes,
Into the sea, the real sea, that seemed
To dwindle, and give up its majesty,
Usurped upon as far as sight could reach.
Meanwhile, the moon looked down upon this shew
In single glory, and we stood, the mist
Touching our very feet; and from the shore
At distance not the third part of a mile
Was a blue chasm, a fracture in the vapour,
A deep and gloomy breathing-place, through which
Mounted the roar of waters, torrents, streams
Innumerable, roaring with one voice.
The universal spectacle throughout
Was shaped for admiration and delight,
Grand in itself alone, but in that breach
Through which the homeless voice of waters rose,
That dark deep thoroughfare, had Nature lodged
The soul, the imagination of the whole.

V.
GROWING UP

The following excerpts (stanzas 9–11) are from the end of Wordsworth's "Immortality" ode. The poem is about growing up to be a man or woman and taking on all the cares of grownups. But it is also about how adults remember the original, imaginative joy of their childhood. Wordsworth thought that all people should keep alive a bit of the child in them as they grow up. (See also lines 7–11 of "My Heart Leaps Up When I Behold" on page 16, which Wordsworth printed at the very top of this poem). The "Immortality" ode is more difficult in language and form than most of the poems in this book, but it is full of famous lines that can be enjoyed almost by themselves. Perhaps the best thing about the poem is the way poet changes back and forth between difficult, "adult" ways of saying things and the simple, vivid thoughts and images of the child who lives in all of us.

Whither is fled the visionary gleam?
Where is it now, the glory and the dream?
　　—from "Ode: Intimations of Immortality," Stanza 4

From Ode: Intimations of Immortality from Recollections of Early Childhood
IX.

If you burn big wood logs in a fireplace and then come back later and stir the charred pieces and ashes, often something is still hot and glowing inside. This is the comparison Wordsworth makes in stanza IX. People may grow up and lose themselves in ordinary work and worries, he says, but stir the "embers," and something still glows brightly—a spark of the first, blazing joy of childhood. Later in the stanza, he changes the comparison: It's as if the vast eternity from which human beings originated were an "immortal sea." Even when we grow old, we have only to close our eyes to remember the waters of eternity—almost like we were children again, laughing and playing on the shore.

O joy! that in our embers
Is something that doth live,
That nature yet remembers
What was so fugitive!
The thought of our past years in me doth breed
Perpetual benediction: not indeed
For that which is most worthy to be blest;
Delight and liberty, the simple creed
Of Childhood, whether busy or at rest,
With new-fledged hope still fluttering in his breast:—
Not for these I raise
The song of thanks and praise;
But for those obstinate questionings
Of sense and outward things,
Fallings from us, vanishings;
Blank misgivings of a Creature
Moving about in worlds not realised,
High instincts before which our mortal Nature
Did tremble like a guilty Thing surprised:
But for those first affections,
Those shadowy recollections,
Which, be they what they may,
Are yet the fountain-light of all our day,
Are yet a master-light of all our seeing;
Uphold us, cherish, and have power to make
Our noisy years seem moments in the being

embers—*the still-hot, glowing pieces of wood or
coal that remain after a fire*
benediction—*blessing*
creed—*belief*
worlds not realised—*unreal or imaginary
worlds*

44

Of the eternal Silence: truths that wake,
     To perish never;
Which neither listlessness, nor mad endeavour,
     Nor Man nor Boy,
Nor all that is at enmity with joy,
Can utterly abolish or destroy!
   Hence in a season of calm weather
     Though inland far we be,
Our Souls have sight of that immortal sea
     Which brought us hither,
   Can in a moment travel thither,
And see the Children sport upon the shore,
And hear the mighty waters rolling evermore.

listlessness—*lacking in energy or spirit*
endeavor—*activity, busyness*
enmity—*hostility*

X.

The beginning of this stanza, with its birds, lambs, tabors, pipes, and old-fashioned way of saying "you" ("ye") is written like a "pastoral" poem, one in which the author pretends to be part of a simple, country world of shepherds. "We in thought will join your throng," Wordsworth says, stepping into something like a Mother Goose world. But he goes on, "What though the radiance which was once so bright / Be now for ever taken from my sight,"—suddenly bringing us into his own personal self, into his mind. Much of Wordsworth's best poetry comes from such a movement between "outside" and "inside" worlds. Later, the poet returns "outside" again to rejoin the world of others—"We will grieve not," he says.

Then sing, ye Birds, sing, sing a joyous song!
    And let the young Lambs bound
    As to the tabor's sound!
We in thought will join your throng,
    Ye that pipe and ye that play,
    Ye that through your hearts to-day
    Feel the gladness of the May!
What though the radiance which was once so bright
Be now for ever taken from my sight,
Though nothing can bring back the hour
Of splendour in the grass, of glory in the flower;
    We will grieve not, rather find
    Strength in what remains behind;
    In the primal sympathy
    Which having been must ever be;
    In the soothing thoughts that spring
    Out of human suffering;
    In the faith that looks through death,
In years that bring the philosophic mind.

tabor—*a small drum*
primal—*original, first*

XI.

"To me the meanest flower that blows can give / Thoughts that do often lie too deep for tears"—these are two of the best-known of Wordsworth's lines. By itself, the thought may seem untrue, or even silly. After all, people pick flowers all the time and children even walk or run over them without anyone wanting to cry. But the lines seem very true coming at the end of this poem, which has worked hard to show how wonderful—even "immortal"—is the spark of life in even the littlest flower, or child.

And O, ye Fountains, Meadows, Hills, and Groves,
Forebode not any severing of our loves!
Yet in my heart of hearts I feel your might;
I only have relinquished one delight
To live beneath your more habitual sway.
I love the Brooks which down their channels fret,
Even more than when I tripped lightly as they;
The innocent brightness of a new-born Day
     Is lovely yet;
The Clouds that gather round the setting sun
Do take a sober colouring from an eye
That hath kept watch o'er man's mortality;
Another race hath been, and other palms are won.
Thanks to the human heart by which we live,
Thanks to its tenderness, its joys, and fears,
To me the meanest flower that blows can give
Thoughts that do often lie too deep for tears.

forebode—*foretell*
severing—*cutting apart, breaking up*
relinquished—*given up*
sway—*power*
fret—*to form a passage by erosion*
palms—*honors*
meanest—*lowliest, most common, most humble*
blows—*blossoms*

47

INDEX